Table of Contents

Where Is the United States?

The United States of America is in North America. It is the third-largest country in the world. The United States' capital is Washington, D.C.

UNITED STATES OF AMERICA

Washington, D.C.

Landforms and Climate

The United States has many landforms.
Mountains lie east and west. Deserts
are in the southwest. A flat plain
is in the middle. Temperatures are
high in summer and low in winter.

Animals

Many kinds of animals live
in the United States.
Mountain lions roam the west.
Bears live in forests. Bald eagles
nest in trees near rivers.

Language and Population

More than 316 million people
live in the United States.
Most Americans speak English.
Some Americans speak Spanish.

Food

Many Americans eat meals with beef, pork, or chicken. Meals are often eaten with potatoes, peas, or corn. Hamburgers and hot dogs are popular too.

Celebrations

On July 4, Americans celebrate

Independence Day.

People fly flags. They watch

fireworks and go to parades.

We the People

15

Where People Work

Most Americans hold service jobs.
Some work in schools, banks,
or hospitals. Farmers grow
corn, wheat, and other grains.

Transportation

Most Americans travel by car.

Travel between cities is common.

Americans travel very long

distances by plane.

Famous Sight

The Statue of Liberty is
in New York City. It stands
305 feet (93 meters) tall.
More than 3 million people
visit the statue every year.

Country Facts

Name: United States of America

Capital: Washington, D.C.

Population: 316,668,567 (July 2013 estimate)

Size: 3,794,100 square miles (9,826,674 square kilometers)

Language: English, Spanish, others

Main Crops: wheat, corn, other grains, fruits, vegetables

Money: U.S. dollar

The United States' flag

Glossary

capital—the city in a country where the government is based

desert—a very dry area of land

fireworks—rockets that make loud noises and display colorful lights when they explode in the sky

grain—the seed of a cereal plant such as wheat, rice, corn, rye, or barley

Independence Day—a national holiday in the United States; Independence Day celebrates the adoption of the Declaration of Independence in 1776; Independence Day is also called the Fourth of July

landform—a natural feature of the land

North America—the continent that includes the United States, Canada, Mexico, and Central America

plain—a large, flat area of land

wheat—a kind of grain; wheat is used to make flour, pasta, and cereal

James, Helen Foster. *Little America*. Bear's Little Series. Ann Arbor, Mich.: Sleeping Bear Press, 2011.

Lindeen, Mary. *Welcome to North America*. Wonder Readers. North Mankato, Minn.: Capstone Press, 2012.

Mitten, Ellen. *My Country*. Rourke Discovery Library. Vero Beach, Fla.: Rourke Publishing, 2011.

Internet Sites

FactHound offers a safe, fun way to find Internet sites related to this book. All of the sites on FactHound have been researched by our staff.

Here's all you do:
Visit *www.facthound.com*
Type in this code: 9781476530741

Super-cool stuff! Check out projects, games and lots more at
www.capstonekids.com

Index

Pebble Books are published by Capstone Press,
1710 Roe Crest Drive, North Mankato, Minnesota 56003
www.capstonepub.com

Library of Congress Cataloging-in-Publication Data
Juarez, Christine, 1976–
    The United States of America / by Christine Juarez.
        pages cm.—(Pebble books. Countries)
    Includes bibliographical references and index.
    Summary: "Simple text and full-color photographs illustrate the land, animals, and people of
the United States of America"—Provided by publisher.
    ISBN 978-1-4765-3514-2 (paperback)
    1. United States—Juvenile literature. I. Title.
    E156.J83 2014
    973—dc23   2013001982

Editorial Credits
Erika L. Shores, editor; Bobbie Nuytten, designer; Wanda Winch, media researcher;
Jennifer Walker, production specialist

Photo Credits
Capstone, 4 (globe), 22 (currency); Capstone Studio: Karon Dubke, 17; Dreamstime: Monkey
Business Images, 13; EyeWire (Photodisc), 15; Shutterstock: Bart Everett, 19, beboy, 1, 7, Dan
Thornberg, 22 (flag), Dennis Donohue, 9, Kamil Macniak, 21, Luciano Mortula, cover, Magnia,
cover, 1 (design element), Orhan Cam, 5, skvoor, 4 (U.S. map), S.Borisov, 11

Note to Parents and Teachers

The Countries set supports national social studies standards related
to people, places, and culture. This book describes and illustrates
the United States of America. The images support early readers in
understanding the text. The repetition of words and phrases helps
early readers learn new words. This book also introduces early
readers to subject-specific vocabulary words, which are defined
in the Glossary section. Early readers may need assistance to read
some words and to use the Table of Contents, Glossary, Read More,
Internet Sites, and Index sections of the book.

Printed in the United States of America in North Mankato, Minnesota.
032013   007223CGF13

Pebble

The United States of America

by Christine Juarez

Consulting Editor: Gail Saunders-Smith, PhD

CAPSTONE PRESS
a capstone imprint